IMAGES
of America

LANCASTER

WORLD WAR I CELEBRATION. After news of victory in Europe on November 7, 1918, thousands of Lancaster citizens crowded Main Street. That evening a huge parade began with the fire department leading. Next the police department marched, then the Civil War veterans, the Spanish War veterans, various organizations, industry workers, and of course the school kids. (Courtesy of Ohio Glass Museum.)

ON THE COVER: **POSING ON MOUNT PLEASANT.** The Schneider family poses for an outing at the very top of Mount Pleasant around 1904. The city can be seen below with the old North School in the background on the far left. One can only hope that father was holding on to the baby with a firm hand. (Courtesy of James Nevins.)

IMAGES
of America

LANCASTER

Connie L. Rutter and
Sondra Brockway Gartner

ARCADIA
PUBLISHING

Published by Arcadia Publishing
Charleston, South Carolina

Library of Congress Control Number: 2010926106

For all general information contact Arcadia Publishing at:
Telephone 843-853-2070
Fax 843-853-0044
E-mail sales@arcadiapublishing.com
For customer service and orders:
Toll-Free 1-888-313-2665

Visit us on the Internet at www.arcadiapublishing.com

GRAND ENCAMPMENT TOWER. In 1902, Lancaster honored the Grand Army of the Republic (GAR) veterans. Arches lined Main and Broad Streets, and a large towering metal structure was erected. The initials on the first arch stood for sons and daughters of Union veterans. A replica of a Civil War soldier stood atop the arch. The sides held oval photographs of Presidents McKinley and Lincoln. (Courtesy of Connie Rutter.)

CONTENTS

ACKNOWLEDGMENTS

As authors, we barely touched on the history of Lancaster. There are so many more people and stories to tell, but there was just no way that we were able to do this in one book. We hope that as readers you find enough to pique your interest, whet your appetite, and encourage you to dig into your local history books to find out more about this amazing town. There are four of the finest museums in the country in the area: the Decorative Arts Center of Ohio, the Georgian, the Sherman Museum, and the Ohio Glass Museum. Visit them all!

Our gratitude and thanks go to Karen Smith, at the Fairfield Heritage Association, for her enthusiasm; Margie Burket and the staff of the Ohio Glass Museum for the gracious use of their extensive Len Hajost photograph collection; Len Hajost for sharing his photographs with the people of Lancaster; James Nevins and his staff at the House of Hearing for their knowledge of Lancaster and the use of their photographs; and to Jack Metcalf for sharing his fabulous postcard collection. Without these wonderful people, this book could not have been written.

We also wish to thank Mary Jane Baltisberger, Robert Evans, and Herman Rutter for the use of additional photographs and research material. It surely made our lives easier.

And special thanks go to our husbands for their patience, support, and sense of humor—they kept us going. And finally we would like to dedicate this book to our children and our grandchildren. Our love for them is immeasurable.

Unless otherwise noted, all images appear courtesy of the authors.

INTRODUCTION

Lancaster, Ohio, with a population of around 35,000, sits snuggled among rolling hills at the base of Mount Pleasant in Fairfield County just a few miles southeast of Columbus. Lancaster was founded on November 10, 1800, by Col. Ebenezer Zane (1747–1811) of Wheeling, Virginia (West Virginia had not been founded yet). Zane is best known for being a merchant, trail blazer, pioneer, and soldier.

A settlement of about 500 Wyandot Indians was located in this region in 1790. Called Tarhe-town, after the principal chief of the tribe, the village was also called Crane-town. The village was located at the bottom of a bluff, which the Wyandot called Standing Stone. Zane settled here and became friends with the natives, and his brother married Chief Tarhe's daughter. Soon after the Treaty of Greenville was signed, Chief Tarhe and many of his tribe moved away and resettled to the northern part of the state in Upper Sandusky. By then, Zane had petitioned Congress to grant him a contract to open a marked trail through Ohio from Wheeling to Limestone, Kentucky, which was a distance of 266 miles. Knowing that this part of the country was ripe for the picking, he requested as compensation three 1-mile square tracts of land located at the river crossings of the Muskingum, Hock-Hocking, and the Scioto Rivers.

The trail opened in 1797 and became known as Zane's Trace. After Zane established a settlement at the base of Standing Stone (now known as Mount Pleasant) just east of the Hock-Hocking River, the settlers began arriving. They came to this beautiful valley and found fertile ground, pure spring water, plenty of game, and timber—all the necessities for making their homes.

Capt. Joseph Hunter emigrated from Kentucky in April 1798 with his family and settled on Zane's Trace. This settlement became known as Hunter's Settlement. After the Hunters arrived and built their cabin, they were joined by Nathaniel Wilson (the elder), John and Allen Green, John and Joseph M'Mullen, Robert Cooper, Isaac Shaefer, and other families.

By the fall of 1800, Zane felt there were enough people wanting to buy his land, so he sent his sons Noah and John, as his attorneys, to lay out a town into lots. Each lot was sold for $5 to $50, and these lots were then divided into numbered squares. Square 16 was to be preserved for a graveyard, a school, and a church. Free lots were to be given to the first tanner, blacksmith, and carpenter who settled and utilized their trades for at least four years. At the request of Emanuel Carpenter, a man from Lancaster, Pennsylvania, the town was named New Lancaster. On December 9, 1800, Ohio governor Arthur St. Clair formed Fairfield County, and in 1805, by act of legislature, the town's name was shortened to Lancaster.

The town grew and began to prosper with businesses and markets. By 1830, Lancaster had a larger population than Cleveland, Ohio. In 1834, the first canal boat came through, and later trains chugged into town over the Cincinnati, Wilmington, and Zanesville (CW&Z) Railroad, bringing to Lancaster even more people and wealth.

The earliest settlers were mostly of German descent from Lancaster County, Pennsylvania. Early settler Judge Jacob Deitrich founded Lancaster's first newspaper, *Der Ohio Adler*, in 1809; the

English version was named the *Ohio Eagle*. The first bank opened on August 30, 1816, and had the authority to issue paper currency, eliminating the use of silver coins. Craftsmen and merchants began opening up shops run by artisans of earthenware, coppersmiths and tinsmiths, saddlers, shoemakers, clock makers, and furniture makers. Soon other buildings sprang up, including a market house, an opera house, a city hall, and the first courthouse.

The most recognizable landmark in Lancaster is Standing Stone, which has been renamed Mount Pleasant. The 250-foot-tall sandstone outcropping has a base of 1.5 miles in circumference, while the apex is only about 30 yards by 100 yards. It is said that the Duke of Saxe-Weimar visited this mount in 1825 and carved his name in the rocks. Another legend tells of abduction and recapture in 1790 of a white woman by the Wyandot Indians. This became the foundation of a novel by Emerson Bennett written around 1848 that has a heroine known as Forest Rose. Lancaster has a Forest Rose Cemetery and a Forest Rose Avenue. Over time, there have been Forest Rose Beer and Forest Rose Flour as well.

The oldest county fair of continuous operation in Ohio was established after natural gas was discovered in February 1887. The fair featured Racing by Gas Light and the Lake of Fire. Today, with over 70 acres, the fair continues to delight people of all ages with the animal barns, horse racing, arts, music, and fair food.

Lancaster has been home to great men and women over the past 200 years. Some were born here and stayed, while others either grew up, went to school, or just lived here for a short time; but all left their mark. And in turn, Lancaster influenced their lives in one way or another.

The one profession that flourished in the early 19th century was the legal system, which produced an abundance of attorneys. Lancaster's location in central Ohio allowed the lawyers to travel the "judicial circuit." It was well known across the country that Lancaster's bar was considered to be the best in the state—if not the nation.

The following is just a small sample of the lawyers, military personnel, and governors who were either born, worked, or lived in Lancaster:

MAJ. GEN PHILEMON BEECHER (1775–1839) was an influential lawyer and judge who immigrated to Lancaster from Virginia. He was a real estate investor, the first president of the Ohio Bank, was elected to the Ohio House of Representatives, and served 10 years in Congress. He was father-in-law to Henry Stanbery and Philadelpus VanTrump and mentor to Thomas Ewing and William Medill, all respected attorneys.

GOV. JOHN BROUGH (1811–1865) was orphaned at the age of 11 and supported himself by becoming a printer's apprentice. He became a newspaper publisher in Marietta, Ohio, and later in Lancaster where he and his brother Charles purchased the *Ohio Eagle*. He presided over of the Cincinnati and Indianapolis Railway and later served as the 26th governor of Ohio. He died while in office.

GOV. JOHN W. BROWN (1913–1993) graduated from Lancaster High School in 1932. After serving in the Ohio Highway Patrol and the U.S. Coast Guard, he began his political career in 1950. He became Ohio's lieutenant governor in 1952 and served as the 58th governor for just 11 days after Frank J. Lausche resigned.

BRIG. GEN. CHARLES EWING (1835–1893) was another son of Thomas Ewing and a brother to Thomas Jr. and Hugh Boyle Ewing. He joined the U.S. Army and was commissioned in 1861. By 1865, he was brevetted colonel and made brigadier general of volunteers the same year.

MAJ. GEN. HUGH BOYLE EWING (1826–1905) was a son of Thomas Ewing. He became an attorney like other members of his family and was later appointed as the U.S. minister to The Hague.

MAJ. GEN. THOMAS EWING JR. (1829–1896) was born in Lancaster to successful lawyer Thomas and Mary Wills Boyle. Ewing was the foster brother and then brother-in-law to William Tecumseh Sherman. He was later promoted to brigadier general, and in 1861 he became the chief justice of Kansas. Although a friend of President Lincoln's, he represented three of the putative Lincoln conspirators in 1865. He was on the defense counsel for Dr. Samuel Mudd and two others accused of the conspiracy to assassinate Pres. Abraham Lincoln.

THOMAS EWING SR. (1789–1871) was an eminent lawyer in Lancaster and the first graduate of Ohio University in 1815. He served six terms in the U.S. Senate, became U.S. secretary of the treasury, and was the first ever U.S. secretary of the interior, a frequent advisor to President Lincoln, and an aid to Daniel Webster.

JAMES A. HILL (1923–) retired in 1980 as an U.S. Air Force general and former vice chief of staff of the U.S. Air Force.

JOHN W. NOBLE (1831–1912) was an attorney and served as U.S. Secretary of the Interior.

GEN. WILLIAM J. REESE (1804–1883) was a lawyer in Lancaster and was married to Mary Elizabeth Sherman, daughter of Judge Charles Sherman.

JOHN G. REEVES (1840– ?) was another attorney born in Lancaster. He was elected as county prosecuting attorney of Fairfield County in 1871 after serving as a captain of Company L, 11th Regiment fighting Native Americans out West.

JAMES SCOTT (? – ?) was a Civil War soldier and the first black man to serve on a Lancaster jury. He was also the first black police officer in the Lancaster Police Department.

MAJ. GEN. WILLIAM TECUMSEH SHERMAN (1820–1891) is Lancaster's most famous son and probably one of the best-known commanders of the Civil War. He was born in Lancaster on February 8, 1820, to Judge Charles Sherman and his wife, Mary. He was raised by Sen. Thomas Ewing after his father died when William was only nine. He eventually married Ellen, the daughter of Ewing. Sherman's military career began after graduating from the U.S. Military Academy at West Point. After retiring from the army in 1884, he made his home in New York City, where he died on February 14, 1891.

HENRY STANBERRY (1803–1881) became the first attorney general of Ohio, was a U.S. secretary of the interior, and the U.S. attorney general. He practiced law with Thomas Ewing and defended Andrew Johnson at his impeachment trial. He was married to Philemon Beecher's daughter.

Over time Lancaster has been home to many entertainers, television and movie celebrities, and other notables:

LLOYD C. DOUGLAS (1877–1951) was the pastor of the English Lutheran Church and rose to distinction in the field of religious writers. He was the author of works that became the hit movies *The Robe* and *Big Fisherman*.

MALCOLM FORBES (1919–1990) was a short-termed Lancastrian. Forbes began his newspaper career in Lancaster, and in November 1947 he dedicated almost the entire issue of his *Forbes Magazine of Business* to Lancaster with an article titled "Free Enterprise—in terms of a Town."

DAVID GRAF (1950–2001) was an actor born in Lancaster. Graf appeared on television in many programs but is best known as Sgt. Eugene Tackleberry in the *Police Academy* series.

ROBERT G. HEFT (1942–2009) was an inventor of sorts. While a student at Lancaster High School in 1958, his history teacher assigned the class to design a new 50-star American flag. The 16-year-old took an old 48-star flag and $2.87 worth of blue cloth and white iron-on material and created the U.S. flag as it is seen today. It was selected by President Eisenhower as the winner. He received a B– for his work.

JAMES HYDE (1962–) is a former fashion model and actor on the daytime television shows *Passions* and *As the World Turns*.

TED H. JORDAN (1924– ?) was an actor on the television show *Gunsmoke* playing the character Nathan Burke.

MARY MURPHY (1958–) is a choreographer who was born in Lancaster. She is a former U.S. champion ballroom dancer and has appeared in several movies. She is now retired from competition and is currently serving as a judge on television's *So You Think You Can Dance*.

WILLIAM RISING (1852–1930) was the son of prominent banker Phillip Rising and his wife, Carrie, and nephew of writer and cartoonist Richard F. Outcault. He became a noted actor in New York City in the early 1900s. Some of his movies included *The Musician's Daughter* (1911) and *Hands Across the Sea in '76* (1911).

RICHARD F. OUTCAULT (1863–1928) was a famous newspaper cartoonist from Lancaster and is known as the "Father of the Comic Strip." Millions of readers have enjoyed his "Buster Brown" comic strips. He also did "The Yellow Kid" cartoons and "Hogan's Alley," which was the first comic cartoon in U.S. newspaper history.

Lancaster also produces first-class athletes. Many have gone on to play college sports and some have even become professional sports figures including:

BOBBY CARPENTER (1983–) is a former Buckeye of The Ohio State University and currently plays professional football for the Dallas Cowboys. His father, Rob, also played professional ball with the Houston Oilers and is currently a coach and teacher at Lancaster High School.

HANK GOWDY (1889–1966) was a professional major-league baseball player and war hero that began his professional baseball career in Lancaster in the Ohio State Baseball League. He was the first active major-league ballplayer to have enlisted with the armed forces during World War I.

JOE OGILVIE (1974–) is a Professional Golf Association (PGA) golfer. His first win was the U.S. Bank Championship in 2007.

Lancaster has one of the most significant historic districts in the Midwest. Known as Square 13, the city offers a walking tour of the area originally designed in 1800. In a 24-block section, 89 buildings have been designated on the National Register of Historic Places. Along with a historic city hall, the area features stately homes, beautiful churches, a bandstand, a fountain, and a Civil War cannon—Sherman's gift to the people for their support and sacrifices during the war.

One

GOVERNMENT AND STREET SCENES

FIRST FAIRFIELD COUNTY COURTHOUSE. The first Fairfield County Courthouse was completed in 1807. The courthouse bell was first brought from Spain to a monastery on the island of San Domingo in the early 1700s. How and why Gen. John Williamson brought it to Lancaster is a mystery. Some people say pirates may have had a hand in it. (Courtesy of the Ohio Glass Museum.)

CURRENT FAIRFIELD COUNTY COURTHOUSE. By 1867, the county commissioners decided the old courthouse was too small for government business and ordered it to be razed. The second and present courthouse, designed and built by Jacob Orman at a cost of around $140,000, was first occupied in 1872. The keystone over one arched doorway is carved with the likeness of Henry Ebner, one of the builders.

NEW CITY HALL. Decked out in all her glory, the new and current city hall is ready for the dedication ceremony in 1898. The magnificent clock tower was originally illuminated by four gas flames. The second floor held both an auditorium and public library. The jail was located in the basement. (Courtesy of Ohio Glass Museum.)

LANCASTER POST OFFICE. The first post office was located in the cabin of Samuel Coats in 1799. During October 1873, over 10,000 letters were mailed from the old post office. The current post office, which is shown here, opened for business on South Broad Street in April 1911.

ENGINE HOUSE NO. 1. Before the Lancaster Fire Department was organized in 1893, fires were fought by the volunteer bucket brigade using leather buckets. By 1853, the first portable hand-pumped engine and hose were bought by the city, and the first steam engine was purchased in 1867. Engine House No. 1 was built in 1899 and still stands on Chestnut Street. Shown are two hook-and-ladder fire trucks in 1815. Today's superior fire department uses the latest in firefighting equipment.

13

CITY HALL AUDITORIUM. Adorned with a curved and ornate ceiling and an elaborate chandelier, the auditorium was located on the second floor of the city hall building. It was the home to many public meetings, music productions, political debates, and entertainment. This photograph was taken about 1900. (Courtesy of Ohio Glass Museum.)

CITY HALL LIBRARY. When Lancaster became incorporated in 1831, the village government was established and the president of the village council served as the chief executive. Isaiah Vorys drafted the plans for the new council chambers in 1887. The city hall also held a public library. This photograph shows the interior. (Courtesy of Jack Metcalf.)

LANCASTER POLICE DEPARTMENT, 1934. Pictured here from left to right are (first row) Charles Hutsler, Chief Gail Sesler, Mayor Charles Moyer, Safety Director Adolph Raab, Capt. George Neeley, and Charles Keeley; (second row) Lawrence Bauer, George Dunkle, Van Hammitt, Lawrence Judy, Charles Douglas, Harley Highley, and Ralph Goodyear. The earliest form of policing was the "property guard" formed when the city was first established. Today Lancaster has an outstanding police department.

FOUNTAIN SQUARE. This photograph, taken in the 1880s at Main and Broad Streets, shows all the action happening in downtown. Seen are the horse-drawn streetcars, Effinger Tavern in the center, and the towers of St. John's Episcopal Church on the right. The steeples of St. Peter's Lutheran Church and the First Presbyterian Church are seen in the background. (Courtesy of Ohio Glass Museum.)

SNOW SCENE. Main Street Hill is viewed before Christmas as wreaths hang from the streetlights decorating downtown. Some businesses during that time included Johnson's Restaurant, Kane Real Estate Company, Isley's Restaurant, and the Liberty Theater (seen on the left). An automobile seems to be stuck in the middle of the street in the snow. (Courtesy of Fairfield Glass Museum.)

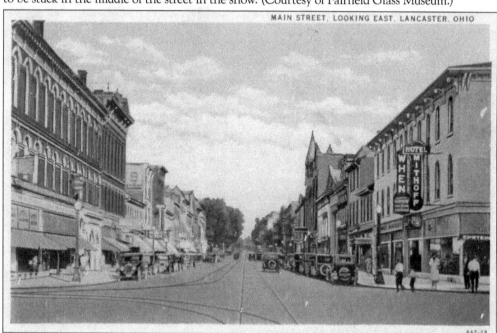

MAIN STREET LOOKING EAST. During the very early days of downtown Lancaster, tree stumps dotted Main Street that were left from the felled trees used for buildings. When any law-breaking citizen was caught and could not pay his bail, he was sent out with a pick and shovel to remove the stumps as his punishment. Here trolley tracks crisscross the intersections. (Courtesy of Jack Metcalf.)

LANCASTER'S OLD CITY HALL. The first city hall was designed by Daniel Sifford, completed in 1859, and sat beside the market house. The three-story building held the mayor's chambers, fire department, a jail, and the local post office. In addition to official business, social gatherings, and church services, lodge and public meetings were also held there. (Courtesy of Ohio Glass Museum.)

BROAD STREET PRIOR TO 1907. This photograph was taken in the summer near where the post office stands today and when horses and buggies owned the streets. Shown in the left background is the Martin Hotel and on the right is the tower of city hall. On the far left is a second-hand store owned by Frank M. Boyer; Boyer boarded in the hotel. (Courtesy of James Nevins.)

17

MAIN STREET. This early 1920s photograph shows the automobiles lining busy Main Street as seen west from Broad Street. Loeher Drugs is seen on the right and the Kresge Building, a bookstore, and the Hotel Kirn are shown on the left. The trolley tracks are seen in the middle of the street. (Courtesy of Jack Metcalf.)

PARKED AUTOMOBILES. Looking down Main Street Hill to Zane Square in the late 1940s, the Clock Restaurant can be seen on the right. During the dinner hour, the restaurant provided organ music. Take note of how the automobiles are parked. On the left, the cars are heading into the curb, and on the right all of the automobiles are heading away from the curb. (Courtesy of Fairfield Heritage Association.)

Two

Businesses of the Past and Present

Davidson Drug Store. Located on East Main Street, this store was the place to go to deliver hawks to be cashed in for a $1 bounty. Dr. Andrew Davidson (from Ireland) and his dog are shown in this *c.* 1900 photograph. At Davidson Drug Store, horse lovers and politicians held their discussions around an old-fashioned pot-bellied stove. (Courtesy of Ohio Glass Museum.)

THE HILLSIDE HOTEL. This residential hotel, razed in 1959, was owned by William and Caroline Bauman Goetz from Germany. It was located on the south side of Main Hill. The hotel became a popular place to hold wedding receptions, and Billy and Callie were always a hit with their music. While Callie sang, Billy played the midget piano—a small keyboard. (Courtesy of Fairfield Heritage Association.)

HOTEL MARTENS. The Martin Hotel was built on the northwest corner of Broad and Chestnut Streets in 1883. In 1905, brothers McCelland and Charles Martens became the owners and changed its name to Hotel Martens (and thus confused many townspeople). The beautiful Victorian hotel with its striking ornate Mansard roof and tower, shown here in the 1960s, was demolished about 1973. (Courtesy of Fairfield Heritage Association.)

Epstein's Shoe Store. All ladies love shoes. In the 1930s, these giggling girls could not wait to find the "perfect pair." Epstein's was just one of the successful businesses owned and operated by local Jewish families. The original store was located in the Smith Building and was founded by brothers Clarence and Charles Epstein in 1916. (Courtesy of Fairfield Heritage Association.)

Mithoff House, 1862. This hotel was the enlarged and remodeled Swan Hotel built in 1861 by Theodore Mithoff, a German immigrant. Mithoff, the president and principal stockholder of the Hocking Valley Manufacturing Company and the Hocking Valley Bank, became even wealthier when a gas well on his property hit it big in 1888. (Courtesy of Fairfield Heritage Association.)

PETER STURGEON ICEHOUSE. Ice taken from the adjoining reservoir is shown going up the incline into the icehouse. The building was erected in the 1870s on what is now known as Markwood Avenue and remained there for 25 years. The two ladies on the right are Rose and Lucy Smith, sisters of Edson B. Smith, a prominent Lancaster gentleman. (Courtesy of Ohio Glass Museum.)

CRYSTAL ICE AND COAL COMPANY. The business was founded in 1910 by John Kilburger and George Brown and was located on Locust Street. Until 1915, all deliveries were made by horse and wagon until they bought the first commercial delivery truck in Lancaster—a chain-driven Republic. Seen here are brothers Russell (left) and Tom Lindsay in July 1916. (Courtesy of Ohio Glass Museum.)

DANISON MONUMENTAL WORKS. The company began carving cemetery head stones and statuary in 1881. Today the business is still in operation and much respected in the industry. In addition to the manual carving, the artists now use lasers to enhance the monuments. In 1948, the business was located at 122 North Columbus Street but now sits across the street from Forest Rose Cemetery.

BROAD STREET LOOKING NORTH. This early 1908 postcard gives a view of the businesses lining Broad Street. (Courtesy of Jack Metcalf.)

C. L. ACKER GROCERY AND CIGAR STORE. The store was located at 118 North Columbus Street in 1904. Grocer Clinton Louie Acker lived with Cora Acker at 218 West Fifth Avenue. (Courtesy of Ohio Glass Museum.)

J. L. DENNY AND COMPANY SHOE STORE. An advertisement for a shoe sale hangs over the door of the boot and shoe company located at 118 West Main Street. The owner and his wife, Harriet, lived at 235 King Street in 1904. (Courtesy of Ohio Glass Museum.)

W. M. KLINGE GROCERY AND BAKERY. William "Bill" Klinge handled the best oysters in Lancaster for years. He always had a special lecture on oysters that he presented to his patrons. The store was located just off West Main Street across from the Mithoff Hotel and next to the City Restaurant. This photograph was taken around 1866. (Courtesy of Ohio Glass Museum.)

SLATER'S HARDWARE. Albert E. Slater was an esteemed builder in town in 1946. His wife, Henretta, wanting a little extra money to spend, convinced her husband to build her a general store. It soon became a hardware and paint store and known as Slater's Hardware. Today the family-operated business is well known for being an old-fashioned hardware store with great service. Shown here is Jon Slater. (Courtesy of Slater's Hardware.)

TOBIAS STUDIOS. Established in 1889, the photography of J. H. Tobias and his two sons, Roy and Lloyd, was considered first class. The award-winning studio was located in the Hotel Martens building. The business was eventually bought by respected photographer Gerald LeVeck. Gerald's son John continues photography today with his own business in Newark, Ohio. (Courtesy of Ohio Glass Museum.)

ZANE SQUARE. Businesses in operation at this location around 1915 included Baus News Agency, Cloud Barber Shop, Baderbaugh Tailors, Wyman Dry Cleaners, and the Reed and Walters Drug Store. (Courtesy of Fairfield Heritage Association.)

WETZEL'S DRUG STORE. Before the days of patent medicines, local druggists recommended remedies for ailments. George Wetzel operated his pharmacy business, which was attached to his residence at 118 East Main Street, for nearly 50 years. The photograph was taken about 1900. (Courtesy of Ohio Glass Museum.)

CLEVELAND PLAIN DEALER. The Lancaster branch of the *Cleveland Plain Dealer* news agency was located at the City News on Fountain Square. This photograph was taken about 1912. (Courtesy of Ohio Glass Museum.)

BLACKSTONE'S FRIENDLY SERVICE STATION. This early 1930s Ford truck advertises Auto-Lite Batteries and is parked next to the Hocking Valley Oil Company. The business was located just south of the railroad tracks where South Broad and South Columbus Streets meet today. At one time, it was also called the Turner Filling Station. (Courtesy of Ohio Glass Museum.)

LANCASTER AUTO GARAGE. These gentlemen pose for the photographer outside the open doors to the garage on Parsons Avenue opposite the Hillside Hotel in 1914. This was a popular place to go and get automobiles repaired. Known as the "Ford Doctor," the boys could repair tires or sell new or used parts and inner tubes for tires. (Courtesy of Ohio Glass Museum.)

HIPPODROME THEATER.
Lancaster once
boasted many theaters,
including this one
located on the north
side of Main Street in
1906; it later became
known as the Liberty
Theater. Over time,
other theaters located
in Lancaster included
the Palace in 1929,
Broad (1938), Princess
(1907), Majestic (1908),
and the Lyric (1913);
the Palace could
seat 1,000 people.
(Courtesy of Ohio
Glass Museum.)

HOTEL LANCASTER, 1940. When Anchor Hocking president I. J. Collins threatened to relocate his factory elsewhere, the chamber of commerce raised $227,000 by selling $100 shares for a new hotel. The redbrick Colonial Revival structure was built on the site of the 1823 Effinger House owned by Samuel Effinger. (Courtesy of Jack Metcalf.)

MARTENS HARDWARE. H. A. Marten established his hardware store in the early 1900s. This photograph, taken in 1915, shows a Titan farm tractor for sale parked out front. The store often exhibited automobiles, tractors, and even a motorcycle in its show window on West Main Street. To the right of the hardware store is the A. J. Kesinger Shoe Store. (Courtesy of Fairfield Heritage Association.)

BARGAIN USED CARS. This car lot, located on South Broad Street, was the place to go for a real bargain. Unlike the automobile businesses of today, a pre-owned vehicle cost less than $200 in 1938. (Courtesy of James Nevins.)

GORDON'S RESTAURANT. One favorite gathering place for good food was Gordon's; here a bowl of soup was 10¢. This photograph was taken about 1917, and the dapper gentleman standing at the counter is Lancaster police officer Gottleib Jurgensmein. "Jurgey," as he was called, was known to visit saloons while on duty. (Courtesy of Ohio Glass Museum.)

GORDON'S SALOON. The original Gordon's was located at 146 East Winding Street. Owner William Gordon is the man in the middle. He and his wife, Katie, lived at 142 East Chestnut Street when this photograph was taken around 1902. (Courtesy of Ohio Glass Museum.)

CLOVER AND SIMON. The business at the corner of High Street and East Sixth Avenue that sold cigars and tobacco during the late 1890s was in the same building that the Farmers Country Store is located today. The shop workers say that the odor of cigar smoke still permeates from the old wooden floorboards of the store. (Courtesy of Ohio Glass Museum.)

WHITE STAR LAUNDRY AND ADAMS EXPRESS COMPANY. This photograph was taken about 1910 and shows delivery wagons from these two businesses parked in front of the White Star Laundry at 209 West Main Street. (Courtesy of Fairfield Heritage Association.)

STABLES OF WILLIAM F. GETZ. The city's first undertaker was Ferdinand Getz. The business was carried on by his two sons under the name of W. F. Getz and Brothers at Columbus Street and Lundy's Lane (now called Fair Avenue). A sideline to the mortuary business was building caskets. In this photograph, a carriage and hearse are parked outside and ready to go. (Courtesy of Ohio Glass Museum.)

McFEE AND MILLER. The ladies' ready-to-wear store was located on the northeast corner of West Main and North Columbus Streets. On the upper floors, the Columbia Commercial University, featuring business education, opened in 1908 and taught professional accountants and stenographers at a cost of $3 per week. This photograph was taken in 1913. (Courtesy Ohio Glass Museum.)

JOSEPH UHL BLACKSMITH SHOP. The shop was located near Davidson Drug Store on East Main Street. Joseph was very well known around Lancaster and served as the blacksmith at the Boy's Industrial School in 1915. The smithy is second from the left wearing his leather apron. The photograph was taken around 1900. (Courtesy of Ohio Glass Museum.)

SNIDER BROTHERS GROCERY AND MEAT MARKET. The Snider boys had a short distance commuting to work; the market was located next to their residence at 849 Columbus Street and was famous for Saturday night grocery-basket drawings. The market had a great location, and it was easy for people to stock up on food for an all-day outing at the fairgrounds just across the street. (Courtesy of Ohio Glass Museum.)

SENNE SHOE FACTORY. Also known as the Lancaster Shoe Company in 1930, the business was located at 230 North Columbus Street at the corner of Mulberry Street. That same year, it employed over 300 workers, and G. F. Lerch was the general manager. The building was later occupied by the Big Bear Company. (Courtesy of Jack Metcalf.)

FAIRFIELD INSURANCE. Shown is a copy of a typical early business card. The Fairfield County Farmers' Mutual Fire Insurance Company was located in the Kirn Building on West Main Street. Take note of the four-digit telephone number. (Courtesy of Jack Metcalf.)

BERRY, BROWN, AND COMPANY. Founded by Philip Rising in 1868 and operated by Abraham Berry and William Brown, the dry goods store continued under that name until 1874. The building, located on the northeast corner of Main and Columbus Streets, was later sold in 1877 to A. Stutson. The building was once known as the Masonic Block. It is seen here in 1870. (Courtesy of Fairfield Heritage Association.)

WILLIAM CLEERY GROCERY, 1910. The grocery store interior seen here was typical of the supermarket of the day. At the store was Forest Rose flour, named for the Lancaster legend. The business was located between Main and Chestnut Streets. (Courtesy of Ohio Glass Museum.)

MUD HOUSE HOTEL. This hotel was located across from the Long Branch Cafe at 146 Winding Street. (Courtesy of Fairfield Heritage Association.)

UNKNOWN TASK. These two gentlemen were busy in the lot next to E. P. Schleicher Grocery located at 121 South Columbus Street. Edward and his wife, Tracie, sold china, glass, and Queensware in addition to the groceries at their store. This photograph was taken around 1916, when the Schleichers lived at 137 East Main Street. (Courtesy of Ohio Glass Museum.)

F. Pfadt. Across the snow-covered Zane Square sits an advertisement for F. Pfadt. Pfadt's was located next to city hall on Main Street Hill. The F. Pfadt and Brothers Produce and Confectionery Store also had a bicycle repair shop within the building. Here a Victorian lady cautiously steps out to cross the street. (Courtesy of Fairfield Heritage Association.)

George Matt Residence. The office and residence of insurance broker George Matt sat on the northeast side of Zane Square in 1898. On the east side of his business (right side of photograph) sat the F. Pfadt Grocery. (Courtesy of Ohio Glass Museum.)

MAIN STREET, 1850. This old photograph shows Main Street with its many shops lining the dirt street. The sidewalks were made of wooden planks, and large stones mark the street corners. On the right is the Samuel H. Bush Foreign and Domestic Grocery. As was the custom of the day, many shopkeepers showed off their wares in front of the buildings. (Courtesy of Ohio Glass Museum.)

JENKS. During the late 1890s, the best place to go for an inexpensive dining experience was Jenk's Lunch Room on South Columbus Street. At the lunchroom, a pork chop or roast beef dinner was 10¢, or for 5¢ more a patron was served sirloin steak or fried ham. The eatery also featured Fox's pies. Here the staff waits behind the counter for hungry customers to arrive. (Courtesy of Ohio Glass Museum.)

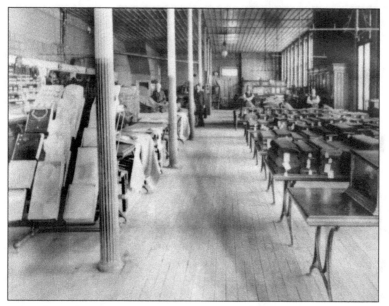

TAILOR SHOP. The Peters and Trout Merchant Tailors shop, a gentleman's clothing store, was located at the Temple of Fashion. Bolts of fabric lay on the tables ready to be chosen to create a new suit. The shirts seen on the display racks are ready to be purchased. The clerks and tailors in the background are waiting to serve shoppers. (Courtesy of Ohio Glass Museum.)

TEMPLE OF FASHION. Peters and Trout maintained a merchant tailoring and clothing shop featuring gentlemen's furnishings and goods. As early as 1830, and until about 1900, the merchant tailoring and the dry goods stores were the core of Lancaster businesses. The men on the second floor are getting a good view of the action below. (Courtesy of Ohio Glass Museum.)

Three

OTHER LANCASTER LANDMARKS

FOUNTAIN SQUARE. After a group of ladies admired a small fountain in the yard of local businessman Andy Bauman, the Fountain Committee Ladies requested that Bauman go to New York and obtain something suitable for the square. A great celebration was held on July 23, 1890, at the dedication. The fountain was cast by J. W. Fiske of New York City and is a copy of a fountain in Nantes, France.

OPERA HOUSE BY NIGHT. Victorian ladies would go the opera house on Chestnut Street for the latest in culture. The gentlemen were not excluded, for the opera house also held frequent wrestling matches. The house was completely remodeled with new electric in-house lighting and new floodlights in 1900. In 1970, the building was razed. (Courtesy of Fairfield Heritage Association.)

CITY HALL, 1900. This postcard of city hall shows the streetcars at the corner of Broad and Main Streets. The Broadway Photography Gallery was located to the right and the City Hall Cafe is just to the left, facing Main Street. The top of the steeples on St. Mary's of the Assumption Catholic Church is shown in the background on the left.

BANDSTAND ON ZANE SQUARE. To celebrate the country's bicentennial, an organization from the Diamond Power Company presented the city with a bandstand. Around 20,000 people attended the dedication, parade, and large fireworks display on July 3, 1976. Today concerts, special events, and even weddings are held there. (Courtesy of Fairfield Heritage Association.)

ROCK MILL, 1906. The combined grist and woolen mill, erected in 1824, is the oldest and largest gristmill on the upper falls of the Hock-Hocking River (named by the Delaware Indians, meaning "Bottle River"). It has six stories above grade level and two below. It was once a gathering place for settlers and a stopping-off place for travelers at the Blue Ball Tavern. (Courtesy of James Nevins.)

CHIEF TARHE. Many say that on the rugged west side of the "Standing Stone" the face of Wyandot chief Tarhe watches over the city. Tarhe, born about 1735, married the captured, red-haired, fair-skinned daughter of Chevalier LaDurante. The chief and many of his tribe members fought beside Gen. William Henry Harrison during the War of 1812. (Courtesy of Fairfield Heritage Association.)

SHERMAN STATUE. An imposing bronze statue of Gen. William Tecumseh Sherman is located in the downtown Veterans Park portion of Zane Square. Cast by world-renowned sculptor Mike Major, the statue was created to celebrate Lancaster's bicentennial in 2000. It was designed to commemorate Lancaster's best-known four-star Civil War veteran.

Children's Home, Lancaster, Ohio.

CHILDREN'S HOME. In June 1813, the Fairfield County Commissioners obtained 28 acres of the Grier property, just east of town, to establish a Fairfield County Orphans' Home. The house had 11 rooms, and the property had two wells and two cisterns. The new Victorian-style building shown here was constructed in 1885 and renamed the Fairfield County Children's Home.

FAIRFIELD COUNTY INFIRMARY, C. 1840. Before the days of Social Security, adults had no place to go when they reached old age and things became more difficult. In 1828, the county constructed a wooden building north of town to house those people. Known as the "poorhouse," it was replaced in 1840 with a much larger brick structure. It now functions as the Fairfield County Board of Health.

SHERMAN MEMORIAL ARMORY. Designed by state architect Karl L. Best and built at a cost of $40,000, construction started in 1914 at 131–135 North Broad Street on property bought from Judge J. G. Reeves. It was used for the local Ohio National Guard until 1950 and then became a public place for exhibits, dances, sport matches, and skating parties. The building was razed in May 1968.

LANCASTER ATHLETIC CLUB, 1922. When the Lancaster elite wanted a place to call their own, they established the Lancaster Athletic Club in 1893 with a bowling alley, gym, meeting rooms, a lounge, and the city's first indoor swimming pool. In the late 1950s, the club was dissolved. The building was razed in 1962. (Courtesy of Jack Metcalf.)

MASONIC TEMPLE, 1908. The Masons began holding their meetings in July 1908 on South High Street in a beautiful building that was once a Methodist Episcopal church. It was used until fire destroyed the structure in December 1944. An exact replica was erected on the same spot and is still being used as their temple. (Courtesy of Fairfield Heritage Association.)

LANCASTER-FAIRFIELD HOSPITAL, 1915. After Dr. George W. Boerstler initiated a bond drive for a hospital in 1914, people voted and approved the amount of $50,000 for a building and $10,000 for furnishings and equipment. The chosen inspirational theme for the bond campaign was "Good Will for the Ill." After opening in 1915, the hospital employed eight nurses and held 36 beds and 10 bassinets.

OLD MARKET HOUSE. The first market house was a frame structure built on the southwest corner of Zane Square in 1810. Here on the second floor, the law-making business of Lancaster was run until the building was razed in 1868. It was here also that Charles Sherman organized the first Grand Commandery of Ohio in the Masonic room. After the second market house was built, city council mandated regulations for operating the market in 1884. The ordinance dictated the hours of operation and required the use of an opening and closing bell. It also stated that no unhealthy animal meat was to be sold or consumed. It even mandated that within one hour of the market closing, the owner's stand or stall must be completely cleaned and his provision or vehicle must be removed. (Courtesy of Fairfield Heritage Society.)

JIMMY'S DRIVE-IN. All the local teenagers growing up in the late 1950s knew about "Jimmy's Jawbreakers." Jimmy Mast opened his first drive-in in 1953 on East Main Street and his second on Memorial Drive the next year. To obtain the famous burger now, one must either attend the county fair or call a hotline number to find out where their portable food wagon is located that day. It could be anywhere!

SKYVIEW CRUISE-IN. Carlos Crum built the first drive-in theater in Lancaster at 2420 East Main Street in 1948. The first film shown was *Sinbad the Sailor*, which cost 50¢ for adults to attend, while kids under 12 years were admitted free. It is still in operation and nostalgic car speakers are available but with state-of-the-art FM stereo sound. Walt Effinger, an employee of 30 years, purchased the theater in 1994.

FIRST COURTHOUSE. The first county courthouse stood in the center of the town square. Seen in the background of this 1865 photograph is the Georgian home to Samuel and Sarah Maccracken. It stands just to the left next to St. John's Episcopal Church. The posters attached to the courthouse advertised the French minstrels performing in town. (Courtesy of Ohio Glass Museum.)

Golf Links and rear view of Country Club, Lancaster, Ohio.

LANCASTER COUNTRY CLUB. When the wealthier residents of Lancaster and members of the athletic club took an interest in golf, they established a country club just south of town in 1909. The golf links and the back section of the clubhouse are shown in this 1915 postcard. (Courtesy of Jack Metcalf.)

Four

CENTURY HOMES AND MUSEUMS

MACCRACKEN HOUSE (THE GEORGIAN). Located in the Lancaster Square 13 Historic District, this 13-room, regency-federal mansion was built by Daniel Sifford in 1833 for Samuel and Sarah Maccracken. Today the home is owned by the Fairfield Heritage Association and stands as a living museum. It is furnished as it might have been in the 1830s with some original pieces. (Courtesy of Ohio Glass Museum.)

REESE-PETERS HOUSE. This Greek Revival structure was built in 1834 for Philadelphian attorney William J. Reese and his bride, Mary Elizabeth Sherman, who was the sister to the Sherman brothers. The home was given to Fairfield County by the Philip R. Peters Trust. In 2000, the completely restored home reopened as the magnificent Decorative Arts Center of Ohio. (Courtesy of Ohio Glass Museum.)

MUMAUGH MEMORIAL. The original Garaghty-Mumaugh House was built about 1805, with the federal section added to the front of the home in 1824. Today it serves as a center for women's clubs and activities. Fannie Mumaugh presented it to the city in 1929. The majestic iron fence is just one of many dotting the historical neighborhoods of Lancaster. (Courtesy of Fairfield Heritage Association.)

OHIO GLASS MUSEUM. After the Ohio House of Representatives officially designated Lancaster as the Pressed Glass Capital of Ohio, the Ohio Glass Museum was established with its mission to foster an appreciation of the heritage of Ohio's glassmaking. The outstanding museum, housed in an old bank, has even incorporated the old vault in its design. A mural of Gen. William Tecumseh Sherman is displayed on the outside of the building.

EWING HOUSE. This beautiful home was built in 1830. Here Thomas Ewing and his wife, Maria Boyle (adopted daughter of attorney Hugh Boyle and niece of Judge Philemon Beecher), raised six children as well as William, one of the sons of his deceased friend, Charles Sherman. Sherman later married the Ewing's daughter Ellen. (Courtesy of Fairfield Heritage Association.)

EFFINGER HOUSE. This federal-style home was built in 1823 by Samuel Effinger, a Virginian who came to Lancaster and became a successful tin and copper smith. The front was added to a stagecoach tavern that later served as the service wing. His son Dr. Michael Effinger, who also lived there, was sympathetic toward African Americans and concealed runaway slaves in the home. (Courtesy of Fairfield Heritage Association.)

CREED HOUSE. This home was built by John M. Creed, a prominent lawyer and Whig politician, in the latest modern Italian style. He also built an underground tunnel from the barn to the basement, which was used for hiding runaway slaves. After Creed died at the age of 38, Darius Tallmadge bought the property and enhanced it by adding the entrance, a tower, and 15 acres of gardens. (Courtesy of Fairfield Heritage Association.)

DENMAN HOUSE. This photograph shows the home in 1930 before extensive renovations were made to the front by the Russell Rising family. This beautiful home was originally built for Henry Stanbery. (Courtesy of Fairfield Heritage Association.)

STANBERY-RISING HOUSE, 1834. This stunning brick Georgian-federal house was built for Henry Stanbery, the law partner of Thomas Ewing. One dramatic point of the house is the hand-carved cornice. It is now owned by the First Methodist Church. (Courtesy of Fairfield Heritage Association.)

McNeil House. In 1860, John D. Martin, who lived in the house now known as the Georgian, had this fine-looking Italianate home built as a wedding present for his daughter and her new groom, Dr. Robert McNeil, a prominent physician in Lancaster. The house is enclosed by another beautifully detailed iron fence. (Courtesy of Fairfield Heritage Association.)

Anchor House, 1834. Daniel Sifford, designer of many Fairfield County structures, built this stately home for Joseph Grubb, a portrait/sign painter and chair builder. It later served as a guesthouse for official visitors to the Anchor Hocking Corporation. The iron fence is from the Devol Foundry, and the entry way is considered by some to be the most beautiful in Lancaster. (Courtesy of Fairfield Heritage Association.)

EDWIN EMBICH RESIDENCE. Edwin, a former teacher, and his wife, Minnie, lived in this stately home where he had his insurance business at 163 West Main Street during the early 1900s. Embich spent about 15 years as a traveling salesman and was known as the "Knight of the Grip." He had an unquestioned reputation as an insurance man. (Courtesy of Fairfield Heritage Association.)

RESIDENCE OF MR. EDWIN EMBICH.

A. J. VORYS RESIDENCE. This house on the south side of the hill at 154 East Main Street was the home to Arthur Vorys and his wife, Jennie. Vorys was an attorney with the Lancaster bar. In 1902, he was appointed to the position of state insurance commissioner. His office was located in the state house. (Courtesy of Fairfield Heritage Association.)

Gen. Sherman's Home, Lancaster, Ohio.

SHERMAN HOUSE. This original three-room saltbox was built in 1811 and is the birthplace and boyhood home of the renowned Civil War general William Tecumseh Sherman and his family. Additions were made to the house in 1816 and again in 1870. Today it serves as a Civil War museum. The home and its furnishings reflect the lifestyle of the Sherman family and features memorabilia of the era. The museum has the distinction of being named a National Historic Landmark. (Courtesy of Jack Metcalf.)

Five

INDUSTRY AND TRANSPORTATION

EMPLOYEES OF THE EAGLE MACHINE COMPANY. To celebrate the 50th anniversary of service to the company, the employees posed for this photograph in front of the factory on December 24, 1930. When the company was located at the corner of Canal and Main Streets in 1890, it manufactured agricultural implements. (Courtesy of James Nevins.)

SHOE WORKERS ON BREAK. Col. Albert Getz established a shoe factory in Lancaster in 1889. By 1900, Henry C. Godman had opened another three factories: the Lancaster Shoe Factory, the Fairfield Shoe Factory, and the Ohio Shoe Factory. These four factories produced 8,000 pairs of shoes a day. Here workers take a break as the men enjoy a cold beer. (Courtesy of James Nevins.)

ELECTRIC COMPANY. Electrical workers stop work and pose for the photographer. This company was established in 1884, and electric light wires were placed on the telephone poles in January 1886. In 1899, just 15 years after the company was started, Lancaster led the rest of Ohio in the use of electricity. That was when they installed the first police call boxes in Ohio. (Courtesy of James Nevins.)

PLANT NO. 1, 1950. With it roots as far back as 1889, the Anchor Hocking Glass Corporation grew to be the second-largest manufacturer of glassware in the world and the largest manufacturer of metal and molded closures for glass containers. By 1950, the company employed some 10,000 workers and boasted net sales totaling some $70,551,108. Most say this plant, located on the west side of town, provided many families with a very nice living.

ANCHOR-HOCKING TABLEWARE SALESMEN. There is no doubt that Hocking Glass, founded by Isaac "Ike" J. Collins, had the biggest impact on Lancaster. Collins began with Ohio Flint before buying the company when it went broke. The glass factories, including the Anchor-Hocking Glass and Lancaster Glass, were at one time the foundation of industry in the town. (Courtesy of Ohio Glass Museum.)

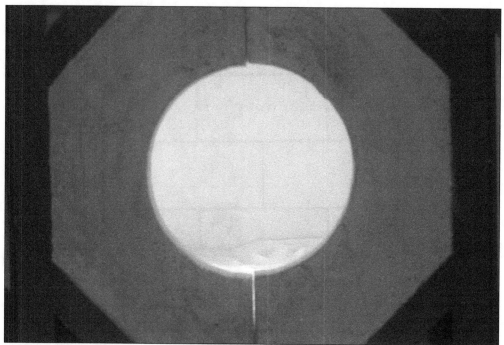

GLASS FURNACE. The interior of the glass furnace in the Ohio Glass Museum glows like the sun. The glass-blowing studio was established so visitors could see the techniques used to create beautiful glass art forms. The museum's glassblower, Mike Stepanski, gives daily demonstrations of his art and even teaches classes on how to blow glass.

GETZ SHOE FACTORY. Just one of four shoe factories in Lancaster, the Getz factory was located at Forest Rose and West Mulberry Streets. This photograph was taken around 1900. The building still remains and stands as an antique mall. (Courtesy of Ohio Glass Museum.)

PLANT No. 1, 2010. By 1950, the Anchor Hocking Glass Corporation owned seven subsidiary companies and 14 manufacturing plants. It had sales offices or manufacturer representatives in 43 cities in the United States and Canada and 8 other foreign cities. The company supplied tableware, dinnerware, glassware, and containers. Today it is still in operation, but the workforce is substantially smaller than in 1950.

RALSTON FOODS. This facility was purchased from General Mills in 1973. Originally built to make snack foods, the plant, located on 119 acres just east of town, currently operates 24 hours a day, seven days a week, and produces ready-to-eat, private-label breakfast cereals. It produces 120 million individual, consumer-packaged units of 25 different cereal products using 130 million pounds of cereal annually.

DIAMOND POWER. The firm started in Detroit, Michigan, in 1903. After consolidating the four plants in Detroit, the company decided to build one plant in Lancaster. After opening the new facility in 1950, it began manufacturing soot blowers, water columns, water-level gages, smoke detectors, illuminators, and utiliscopes. The first president at the Lancaster plant was Willis P. Thomas.

RBM/FAIRFIELD INDUSTRIES. Ivan Reddinger, William Ball, and Wallace Morris founded the RBM Company in 1922. In 1947, they chose the site of the old Godman Shoe Factory at the corner of Columbus and Mulberry Streets to become the RBM Division of the Essex Wire Corporation. Here they made switches for automobiles. Today the building stands empty.

Transportation on Main Street. A variety of transportation modes can be seen in this postcard from 1914. Trolleys, wagons, and automobiles all line the street. (Courtesy of Jack Metcalf.)

Horses and Buggies. Unlike today, this old postcard reflects the softer side of living in the early 1900s, when traffic was not congested and parking was readily available. (Courtesy of Jack Metcalf.)

CHESAPEAKE AND OHIO FREIGHT HOUSE. This photograph was taken around the early 1960s. The freight building currently houses a museum. (Courtesy of Ohio Glass Museum.)

STATE FARM CAR. The Boys' Industrial School was once called the State Farm. Sitting at the railroad crossing at South Broad Street, the railroad car was heavier than regular cars, which enabled it to push coal cars from town to the school. The name of State Farm was changed in 1885. At one time, it was also called the Fairfield School for Boys. (Courtesy of James Nevins.)

CANAL FACTORIES. The Lateral Canal was not started in Lancaster until 1832 after a group of local businessmen raised the money to get it going. This photograph shows the tobacco warehouses that lined the Hocking Canal. Other warehouses, iron foundries, and mills were built. The canal was located where Memorial Drive is today and was drained in 1894. (Courtesy of Fairfield Heritage Association.)

HOCKING VALLEY DEPOT, 1915. The "iron horse" came to Lancaster on April 11, 1854, at 4:30 p.m. as 8,000 enthusiastic fans waited to welcome the first train from the Cincinnati, Wilmington, and Zanesville Railway Company. As the train arrived, it was greeted by cheering crowds, waving flags, and a blaring band. The festivities were followed by dining and dancing with great celebration.

Handcar, c. 1910. The section crew from the Hocking Valley Railroad brought their handcar to a standstill long enough for their picture to be taken. (Courtesy of Ohio Glass Museum.)

Last Trolley in Lancaster. Hundreds of people line the street at the corner of Broad and Main Streets to witness the last day of the streetcars. Like many other cities during this time period, Lancaster too lost the trolley business to the advent of city buses. Just a few years later, the buses, in turn, lost out to privately owned vehicles. (Courtesy of James Nevins.)

Six

PARKS AND SCHOOLS

SKATERS IN RISING PARK. As a Christmas present in 1908, Philip and Carrie Rising presented to the City of Lancaster 73 acres of land at the foot of Mount Pleasant, now known as Rising Park. The gazebo near the pond was built in 1990 by friends and family in honor of the Risings' grandson George R. Rising. Here skaters enjoy twilight time on the pond.

BURNT CORKERS. This group was established in 1941 to put on minstrel shows; it lasted until 1959. The name was derived from burning corks and applying the residue to faces to obtain the "black face" appearance. Other minstrel groups included Lancaster Hottentots, Dixie Doodles, and the Hooligans. This photograph shows a reunion of the Burnt Corkers at Rising Park.

MILLER PARK. A gift of 23.8 acres of land at West Sixth Avenue and North Memorial Drive from Charles and Julia Hutchinson became the site of Lancaster's municipal swimming pool. Given in the memory of Frederick Miller in 1922, the land was the second choice for the pool, which opened in 1923. The first choice of the people, Rising Park, was turned down by the park board. (Courtesy of Jack Metcalf.)

BIS ADMINISTRATION BUILDING, 1909. The Boys' Industrial School (BIS) was situated on 1,170 acres south of town. The facility closed in 1963 but reopened one year later as a correctional facility for adult offenders and renamed the Southeastern Ohio Correctional Institution. This building contained offices, reception rooms, parlors, dining rooms, residences, guest rooms, a council chamber, and a telegraph office.

GREENHOUSE. The conservatory at the BIS provided a place for the growing of flowers and vegetables. What began as a few log buildings grew into a small city. In addition to school education, the boys were also taught the trades. The facility also maintained a shoe and boot factory, a brush factory, a tailor shop, and a cane seat-making department. (Courtesy of Mary Jane Baltisberger.)

WHITE CHAPEL AT THE **BIS.** Religious services were held every Sabbath. One famous person who spent time at the BIS as a child was Bob Hope. After becoming an adult, he donated sizable sums of money for the upkeep of the facility. Ladies standing in front of the stone church are dressed in their Sunday best. (Courtesy of James Nevins.)

No. 807.   Buildings at the Boys Industrial School, Lancaster, Ohio.

BUILDINGS AT THE **BIS.** Other buildings on the grounds included a laundry and washhouse, water tower, bake house, stables, coal houses, hospital, icehouse, mending room, engine room, knitting room, piggery, and chamber of reflection. The grounds were beautifully landscaped with a lily pond, gravel drives, flower houses, and grass lawns with trees and flowers. (Courtesy of Jack Metcalf.)

JENNINGS HALL, 1909. The Ohio government established the Ohio Reform School, the predecessor of the BIS, for boys between the ages of 8 and 18 in 1857. The first 10 boys came in 1858. They maintained an "open system" of detainment, and by 1901 twenty-eight other states had adopted this same operation for their juvenile prisons. Jennings Hall was the drill hall and gymnasium. (Courtesy of Jack Metcalf.)

PUMP STATION AND ARTESIAN WELLS. The reform school was a completely sustainable facility. Here the boys spent half a day in school and the other half working on the farm or learning a trade. All boys were required to do military training as part of their penitence. This photograph was taken about 1909. (Courtesy of Jack Metcalf.)

DRILL TEAM. It was very popular in the early 1900s for people to ride the interurban (Fairfield Traction Company) to the BIS on a Sunday afternoon to see the cadet dress parade. Here the drill team members use Springfield rifles during squat-thrust exercises on the school grounds. (Courtesy of Ohio Glass Museum.)

ARTILLERY PARK, 1912. In front of the cannon in the park is a bathtub-shaped vessel with water coming from a pump. Early history proved that the BIS was a complete success. The superintendent estimated that over 80 percent of the boys had turned out very well. After 20 years of operation, over 3,170 boys had been detained there at one time or another, but at that point only 514 were in attendance. (Courtesy of Jack Metcalf.)

CORN FIELDS. The boys were expected to work on the farm that produced food for the kitchen. The state established a canning facility at the school in 1915 to preserve as much food as possible. The boys even processed their own ketchup, made sauerkraut, and grew fruit trees and crops.

SCHOOL GROUNDS, 1909. This postcard shows the gravel walkways and beautifully landscaped grounds of the Boys' Industrial School. (Courtesy of Jack Metcalf.)

SUPERINTENDENT'S RESIDENCE AT BIS. There were nine two-story brick family buildings with a basement. Located there was the washroom and play area for the boys; the second story was the schoolroom and apartments for the elder brother (officer) and his family. With only a few exceptions, the officer's wife was the teacher. The third story was the sleeping apartment for the boys.

NEW LANCASTER HIGH SCHOOL. Construction began on the second high school in 1961 on a 75-acre field just north of town. Completed in 1963, it also housed a planetarium, which was constructed with money donated from the widow of Phillip Rising Peters. This was given in memory of her husband and son. She also donated the instruments and equipment used in the facility.

LANCASTER HIGH SCHOOL. This building was erected in 1905, and boasted 10 classrooms, physics and chemistry laboratories, both boys and girls locker rooms, a gymnasium, auditorium, and cafeteria. The number of students outgrew the space, and a new high school was built.

WEST SCHOOL. The first school on the west side of Lancaster was in this small school building at the corner of Washington and Seventh Avenue. The beginning salary for teachers at that time was around $35 a month for nine months. This building eventually became a church. A new West School building was erected at the corner of Garfield and Sixth Avenues in 1904.

WEST SCHOOL BUILDING, CORNER DESHLER AVENUE AND THURMAN STREET

OLD NORTH SCHOOL. The first North School was located on the northeast corner of Mulberry and Broad Streets in 1849. A new North School was built on the corner of Broad and Allen Streets in 1873; Lancaster High School was located on the second floor. Take note of the young girls standing in the windows. (Courtesy of Fairfield Heritage Association.)

SECOND NORTH SCHOOL. The Lancaster School Board secured 4.75 acres between Broadway and Allen Streets for the second North School building, and the construction was completed in 1873. It was used until the next new building was completed in 1917. (Courtesy of James Nevins.)

FIRST ST. MARY'S SCHOOL. The school, built in 1841, was located at the corner of High and Chestnut Streets beside the church. The three-story building had a basement, commodious second floor, and a third floor that held primary grade classrooms. The high school was added in 1891. The building was later torn down and replaced in 1923 by the rectory. (Courtesy of Ohio Glass Museum.)

BASKETBALL TEAM.
This photograph,
taken in 1926,
highlights the
St. Mary's team.
(Courtesy of
James Nevins.)

79

WEST SCHOOL. The seventh and eighth graders of Professor Welk pose in front of the West Building in Lancaster. The girls far outnumber the boys. (Courtesy of James Nevins.)

OHIO UNIVERSITY CAMPUS. Established educational institutions were part of the settlement of the Northwest Ordinance of 1787. Ohio University was located in Athens in 1804. The first two graduates in 1815 were both from Lancaster. Fifty years ago, it extended services to Lancaster. Today over 2,000 students attend the Lancaster campus annually.

SECOND SOUTH SCHOOL. After the first South School building was razed, this one was constructed and opened in 1875 at a cost of $30,000. It held 12 rooms. The general contractors were the Vorys brothers. This photograph was taken shortly before the building was demolished in 1930. (Courtesy of Fairfield Heritage Association.)

SOUTH SCHOOL. The current building was erected in 1931 using the popular yellow-colored brick found in many schools around the city. The old school bell, purchased in 1867 and used in the second South School building, was incorporated in the design. The building cost around $158,000, and the Parent-Teacher Association purchased the radio and sound system, the grand piano, and the wire fencing surrounding the playground.

St. Mary's School. The new St. Mary's Parochial School building was formally opened on the afternoon of Saturday, September 7, 1907. The ladies sold souvenir paperweights in the main hall, and sandwiches, ice cream, and cake were served. The building was formally dedicated on the following Monday morning by Bishop Hartley. The school cost roughly $35,000 and stands today on Chestnut Street.

NORTH PRIMARY SCHOOL REAR MAIN BUILDING BROADWAY

North Primary School. The school board erected a new building just north of the new North School for African American students in 1849 at a cost of $1,300. It was a neat, one-story brick structure divided into two compartments that held both primary and grammar grades. The students had all the same benefits as white students. The arrangement of this separate school system was abolished in 1886.

Seven

Fairgrounds, Campgrounds, and One Standing Stone

LANCASTER FAIRGROUNDS. Shown is the oval dirt track at the base of Standing Stone. Cheering audiences have seen many horses race around the track since the fair was established. The fairgrounds have also been home to some famous people and events. In 1966, Pres. Lyndon B. Johnson spoke there in support of the Vietnam Conflict. (Courtesy of Jack Metcalf.)

AT THE BASE OF MOUNT PLEASANT. The first Fairfield County Fair was held on John Reeber's farm in 1861. Reeber and a few other farmers organized the Fairfield County Agriculture Society. Since then, the annual fair has always been held in October. Most of the time, the beautiful changing colors of the autumn leaves set the stage for the fair; other times snow flurries do. (Courtesy of James Nevins.)

ADVERTISING POSTER. Races were once held at night and illuminated by the brilliant light of natural gas from large standpipes inside the oval. The theme of the promotional material in 1889 was the romance of the legendary Forest Rose. (Courtesy of James Nevins.)

CATTLE SHOW. A favorite part of any county fair for some people is visiting the cattle barns. This photograph shows the steer judging in 1913. The men in the crowd seem to be picking their own winners. (Courtesy of Ohio Glass Museum.)

CIVIL WAR CAMP. This photograph was taken during the Civil War and shows the Lancaster Fairgrounds being used as Camp Anderson. The tents are pitched behind the judges' stand. (Courtesy of Fairfield Heritage Association.)

HORSE RACING. To many fairgoers, the highlight of the county fair is horse racing. This photograph shows the crowd "riding the rails" and cheering for their favorite sulky rider. Many people, unaware of the odds of the horses, cheered for the driver with the best-colored silks or just based on the looks of the horse. (Courtesy of Ohio Glass Museum.)

No. 800. Fair Grounds and Mt. Pleasant, Lancaster, Ohio.

PARADE REST. Many bands have performed at the fairgrounds since it was established. This postcard shows a military band with soldiers at parade rest in the background. The photograph was taken around 1914. (Courtesy of Jack Metcalf.)

FAIRGROUNDS. On the right side of this photograph are two white poles, which were standards to support bulletin boards for advertising posters. On the far right is Kinkead Hill with the natural gas derrick. The three-story building is the ladies' grandstand, and the men's grandstand is on the left. To the far left are the art hall and the horse stables. (Courtesy of Ohio Glass Museum.)

TRAINING CAMP. During the Civil War, training camps were set up at local parks and open fields. In Lancaster, the fairgrounds were utilized and temporarily renamed Camp Anderson. This 1860s photograph shows the tents and campsites of the soldiers. (Courtesy of Ohio Glass Museum.)

POST OFFICE. The Methodist Campground, established in 1877, was so popular during the early 1900s that it had its own bookstore. The grounds became a small village with a post office that stood for over 65 years. This photograph was taken about 1906. (Courtesy of Jack Metcalf.)

METHODIST CAMPGROUND, 1877. This facility is located on West Fair Avenue and once had a hotel, an auditorium, and many individual cottages. Speakers that have visited there include William Jennings Bryan in 1920, Drs. Norman Vincent Peale and Charles A. Tindley, and preacher Billy Sunday. They spoke to large crowds in the auditorium, which was built in 1896 and seated over 2,000 people.

SUMMER TIME. Many visitors came to the Methodist Campground, including William McKinley before becoming president. And many circuit-riding preachers came there to preach against the sins of alcohol. In 1842, local banker John M. Creed and Dr. M. Z. Kreider organized a chapter of the Washington Temperance Society. This photograph was taken about 1912. (Courtesy of Jack Metcalf.)

WOODSIDE HOTEL. Built in 1887 on the north side of the Methodist Campground to serve the railroad traffic, it was removed board by board and rebuilt on the south side of the campground in 1918 to take advantage of the automobile traffic. This photograph was taken around 1910. It now serves as a museum and the Lancaster Campground Hall of Fame.

GATHERING. Many reunions, parties, band camps, and drama plays have gathered at the Methodist Campground over the years. Here a group of young ladies gathers for a photograph under the trees in 1939. A few older ladies, as well as a nurse and a couple of gentlemen, are seen standing among the teenagers. (Courtesy of Jack Metcalf.)

REFURBISHED WOODSIDE HOTEL. This photograph shows the hotel's appearance after it was moved to the other side of the campgrounds. The third floor was removed, and the large porches were put on using the recycled wood.

SHELTER HOUSE. Work on the stone shelter house at Rising Park began in 1939 and was a project established as a relief measure by executive order. The Works Progress Administration (WPA) was then transferred to the Federal Works Agency in 1939 and offered work to unemployed Americans. The building was completed by the Lancaster Park Board about 1940. (Courtesy of Jack Metcalf.)

BIRD'S-EYE VIEW. In this photograph, taken around 1938 from the top of Mount Pleasant, the photographer had a view of the city in all directions. (Courtesy of Jack Metcalf.)

PARTY TIME. This group of young people enjoys the afternoon on Mount Pleasant. It was a common occurrence for parties to be held atop the hill in the early 1900s. Many of the parties were moonlight picnics with Japanese lanterns glowing in the night sky. (Courtesy of James Nevins.)

YOUNG LOVE. Mount Pleasant was just the place to take a date on a Sunday afternoon. Here the young gentleman gives his lady a view of the city below. (Courtesy of Jack Metcalf.)

Eight

FRIENDS, FAMILY, AND PEOPLE OF DISTINCTION

MR. PHILLIPS. Alexander Phillips, a glassworker who resided in the village of Cedar Heights on the west side of Lancaster, rocks on his porch at 514 Pierce Avenue. According to the description on the back of the image, he is sitting here listening to music playing on his long-horned gramophone while the neighborhood children work in his garden. The photograph was taken about 1904. (Courtesy of James Nevins.)

WELCOMING HOME THE HEROES. Crowds of friends and family welcome the Spanish-American War veterans returning home in 1898. Behind the train is the African Methodist Episcopal Church located on Walnut Street. It was erected in 1869, and in 1914 the building was turned around to face the street. (Courtesy of Ohio Glass Museum.)

KIDS PARADE, C. 1900. Playing at the intersection of West Mulberry Street and Forest Rose Avenue, these children have formed a band with drums, a horn, and a flag. They added paper hats to complete their uniforms. (Courtesy of Ohio Glass Museum.)

YOUNG BOYS BAND. As part of the discipline and recreation of the Boys' Industrial School, participation in a marching band was offered to the young men staying there. At one time, the band had 42 members. Here the band poses in front of the administration building. (Courtesy of Jack Metcalf.)

SOCIAL LODGE. Secret Societies were popular during the early 1900s. Among these were the Knights of Honor, Independent Order of Odd Fellows, Knights of St. George, Temperance Movement, and the Lancaster Commandery of Knights Templar. Here the Knights of Pythias chapter is meeting and camping at Rising Park in Lancaster. The banner states, "Leon Company No. 9." (Courtesy of the Ohio Glass Museum.)

SOUTH SCHOOL CLASS. Children pose for Miss Patrige's first-grade class at South School in 1922. It appears that Miss Patrige had her attention on something other than the photographer. (Courtesy of James Nevins.)

CEDAR HEIGHTS GRADE SCHOOL. Shown is the second-grade class in 1949. A burst of industry in the early part of 1900 brought a growing population to the area and to city schools. In 1904, the Utica School was built, and in 1913 the new Cedar Heights building was erected just south of the Hocking Glass west side plant. This is the second Cedar Heights School building.

TEA PARTY. This tea party was held on North Columbus Street with Mrs. Edson B. O. Smith and her sister. Smith was a prominent local jeweler and amateur photographer. (Courtesy of Ohio Glass Museum.)

FAMILY PORTRAIT, C. 1948. Posing for the camera in the backyard of their home at 200 Sherman Avenue are William Higginbotham, his wife Opal, and children (from left to right) William, Connie, and Ruth. William worked as a section hand on the Chesapeake and Ohio Railroad in Lancaster.

ST. MARY'S HIGH SCHOOL BASKETBALL TEAM, 1924–1925. St. Mary's of the Assumption parish opened an elementary school in 1841 on the third floor of the church building. After the new church opened in 1854, the old building became the school. In 1891, a high school was added to the school. (Courtesy of James Nevins.)

YOUNG BASEBALL PLAYER. Known only as Robbie, this young player was dressed for sport in his quilted pants and high stockings in 1900. (Courtesy of Ohio Glass Museum.)

FOOTBALL TEAM. Lancaster has produced many great college and professional football players since the school began. Probably the most famous are professional players Bobby Carpenter and Rex Kern. These handsome young men are from the class of 1910 at Lancaster High School.

CARS GATHERED. The Cincinnati Chamber of Commerce was touring Lancaster during 1913. This photograph shows them visiting the site at Main and Broad Streets looking north to the railroad tracks.

LAYING STEPS, 1897. City hall workers pose during the final construction phase of the new city hall as the steps were being installed. The only man identified is Ed Fricker, who stands in the third row, second from the left. (Courtesy of Fairfield Heritage Association.)

GUARDSMEN. Victorian men were very social. They belonged to private clubs ranging from literary to military inspired. The local militia was organized in 1881 by Capt. Albert Getz, founder of Lancaster's first shoe factory. It was first known as the Sherman Light Guards and later renamed the Mount Pleasant Guards. Here the local National Guardsmen drill as they march with Krag-Jorgensen rifles.

BANQUET. These young men from Phi Sigma Chi Inc. enjoy a banquet to celebrate the Feast of the White Carnation just before Christmas on December 8, 1930. (Courtesy of James Nevins.)

PHILIP RISING. Rising, a member of Lancaster society, was a banker and capitalist. His son William S. was a celebrity in New York City during the early 1900s. (Courtesy of Fairfield Heritage Association.)

ROBERT HEFT AND FRIENDS. Just before his death in 2009, Robert G. Heft (center front), designer of the 50-star American flag, met with friends. Pictured with Robert from left to right are Cindy Prince, Bill Sisco, and Yvonne Lorenz. (Courtesy of Bill Sisco.)

BASEBALL TEAM. This motley crew poses for a team shot. By the looks of the condition of their uniforms, one would think the photograph was taken after a long, dirty game. (Courtesy of Ohio Glass Museum.)

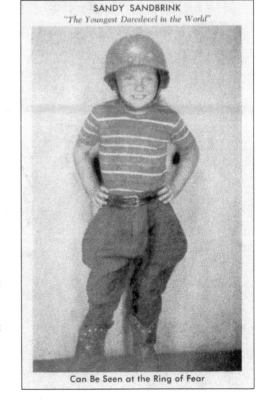

SANDY SANDBRINK
"The Youngest Daredevil in the World"

Can Be Seen at the Ring of Fear

LITTLE DAREDEVIL. Young "Sandy" Sandbrink had been riding with his grandfather for two and a half years when this photograph was taken. He rode standing on one narrow, 3-foot board in a steel, cage-like contraption called the Ring of Fear while the motorcycle he was on traveled at a speed of almost 60 miles per hour. He was born in Lancaster in 1952.

YOUNG LADIES. Eleanor Reed Fisher (right) was a young lady that often visited the Boys' Industrial School and the Lancaster Campground. She is shown standing in front of the hotel at the campground in 1925 when she was 19 years old. She later married George Tabit; she passed away in 1967. (Courtesy of Mary Jean Baltisberger.)

PONY CART. Little Edna Mae Hunter, age seven, takes a ride in her cart pulled by her pony. Edna lived on Washington Avenue as a young girl.

UNKNOWN GLASSBLOWER. Many glassblowers worked at Lancaster Glass. Some workers began as apprentices as early as the age of 15, and occasionally people spent their whole careers hand-blowing glassware. (Courtesy of Ohio Glass Museum.)

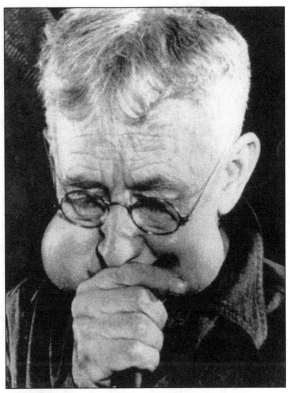

HOCKING H. HUNTER. Hocking H., son of Capt. Joseph and Doretha (Berkshire) Hunter, was the first white child born in Fairfield County on August 23, 1801. After being admitted to the bar in 1824 and serving as prosecuting attorney of Fairfield County, he was later elected judge of the Supreme Court of Ohio. He married Ann Matlock in 1823, fathered nine children, and died on February 4, 1872.

GENERAL SHERMAN. Sherman is believed to be the only eminent American named for an American Indian chief. His friends and family called him "Cump." The graduate of West Point married Ellen Ewing, the eldest daughter of his friend and benefactor Thomas Ewing. After retiring from the army, he moved to New York City, where he later died. He is buried in Calvary Cemetery, St. Louis. (Courtesy of Fairfield Heritage Association.)

WILLIAM TECUMSEH SHERMAN (1820–1891). Surrounded by other Civil War dignitaries and American Indians is Lancaster's most distinguished son—Gen. William Tecumseh Sherman. Born to Judge Charles Robert and Mary Hoyt Sherman, he was taken in by his father's good friend and neighbor, Thomas Ewing, after his father died unexpectedly when Sherman was nine years old.

TELLA EFFINGER. The daughter of Dr. Michael and Elmira (Catlin) Effinger, born in Lancaster, was a lady of finished education and fine accomplishments. She entered Troy Seminary in 1866 and left in 1867. The same year, she married Charles Convers Duncan. She and Charles had four children. In 1894, she was living in Washington, D.C. (Courtesy of Fairfield Heritage Association.)

DR. GABRIEL MIESSE JR. Born in 1838 to Gabriel Miesse Sr. and Mary (Wiest) Miesse, he became a physician, surgeon, musician, composer, and music teacher. At 13, he established a menagerie of native animals, birds, reptiles, fish, geological specimens, and American Indian relics and performed for P. T. Barnum. By 16, he was giving musicals and anatomy lectures. (Courtesy of Fairfield Heritage Association.)

CHARLES SHERMAN. Judge Charles Sherman migrated from Connecticut and became a local attorney. He fathered 11 children, including William Tecumseh, John, Charles, and Mary. He served as a tax collector in Lancaster and as an Ohio Supreme Court justice. He died at age 42 from cholera, leaving his wife alone to raise the children. (Courtesy of Fairfield Heritage Association.)

JOHN SHERMAN, (1823–1900). John was the son of Charles and Mary Sherman. He became a U.S. senator, congressman from Kansas, U.S. secretary of the treasury, U.S. secretary of state, and the author of the Sherman Anti-Trust Act. (Courtesy of Fairfield Heritage Association.)

GOV. WILLIAM MEDILL (1802–1865). Medill was elected by the Democratic Party to serve as the 22nd governor of Ohio in 1853. As a distinguished lawyer from Lancaster, he served as president of the Ohio Constitutional Convention, was member of the Ohio legislature, and was a U.S. congressman. He also served as an Indian Agent in Washington, D.C. His monument stands in Elmwood Cemetery.

HUNTER FAMILY. The Eli Hunter family poses for a group shot. Pictured here are, from left to right, (first row) Eli Curtis Hunter and wife Susannah Poling Hunter; (second row) Clara, Stella, Emma, and Dora May; (third row) George, John, Lewis, Amos, and Osea.

REX KERN (1949–). Rex William Kern is a former professional football player who graduated from Lancaster High School and played as an Ohio State University Buckeye on the 1968 National Championship team. He was elected to the College Football Hall of Fame in 2007. (Courtesy of Chance Brockway Jr.)

KATIE SMITH (1974–). Smith, born in Lancaster, was named the Gatorade National Basketball Player of the Year during her senior year in high school. Awards she has earned include the Big Ten MVP (1996), five-time WNBA All-Star, and Olympic gold medal winner in 2000, 2004, and 2008. She has played for the Columbus Quest, the Minnesota Lynx, and the Detroit Shock. (Courtesy of Karen Goodin.)

Nine

EVENTS TO REMEMBER

DEDICATION. Hundreds showed up for the dedication ceremony of the new city hall. With financing made possible from the profits of the natural gas deposits and a bond issue, the building was erected in 1898. It was designed by Chicago architect Henry Ives Cobb. The Romanesque building was constructed from local sandstone. (Courtesy of Ohio Glass Museum.)

AIR SHOW. The local Elks Club sponsored an air show in August 1912 at the fairgrounds. Onlookers from the top of Mount Pleasant and in the crowded grandstand were mesmerized when a Curtiss Aeroplane swooped over the racetrack. Everyone escaped injury when one plane nearly crashed after hitting a fence, snapping a guy wire, and breaking one of its wheels. (Courtesy of James Nevins.)

FEBRUARY 22, 1897. The laying of the cornerstone ceremonies held on a cold, rainy day in winter still brought out many people to the new city hall. Seen in the upper right-hand corner is a steam laundry, and next to that is a known house of "ill repute." (Courtesy of James Nevins.)

SNOWFALL. During November 1950, a snowstorm dumped over 25 inches of snow on the town. This photograph shows how Main Street was decorated for Christmas with garland hanging across the street. At that time, the city had no snowplows, so at the request of the mayor hearty men throughout the city took shovels in hand and did the job themselves. (Courtesy of James Nevins.)

STAGECOACH. These people are having a great time riding atop the horse-drawn stagecoach in the Lancaster sesquicentennial celebration. The huge parade, held on June 10, 1950, was just one of many events commemorating the 150th birthday of the city. (Courtesy of James Nevins.)

VETERANS PARADE.
The crowd in this photograph is lining the street in 1898 to celebrate the end of the Spanish-American War. The veterans were met with a parade. One account of the event stated, "Cannons boomed, factory whistles screamed, bells clanged, and spectators cheered."

PARADE. As in other conflicts, when called to duty Lancaster gave her all. The Lancaster Mount Pleasant Guards, Company I, served as occupational troops in Puerto Rico during the Spanish-American War. Lancaster also loved to show appreciation to the troops with parades. The tradition has not changed, as parades are still loved by everyone. (Courtesy of James Nevins.)

OHIO STATE FOOTBALL. There is never any event more important in Ohio than an Ohio State University football game. Here No. 42, Bobby Carpenter from Lancaster, displays his sporting talent on the field during a game in Ohio Stadium. (Courtesy of Chance Brockway Jr.)

DECORATED TROLLEY. Before electric trolley lines were installed, streetcars were horse drawn. Cars lined up to handle the great number of people wanting to go to the fair in 1890. On busy days, superintendent Andy Bauman brought in extra cars from other cities. The horses were kept in the stables on Main Street, where the trolleys were stored when not in use. (Courtesy of Ohio Glass Museum.)

TROOPS. Friends and family swarm the train depot to welcome home the Spanish-American War veterans on South Broad Street. The white building across the railroad tracks is the Red Onion Inn.

BUFFALO BILL. The drivers of local grocery delivery wagons sit outside a local hotel in 1911. Posted on the side of the building is a large sign announcing the arrival of Buffalo Bill and his Wild West Show on June 14. (Courtesy of James Nevins.)

FLOOD OF 1948. Disaster in the form of water has struck Lancaster many times. One of the worst happened in 1948, when 8- to 10-foot floodwaters hit the west side. On the left is the Gay-Fad Studio on Pierce Avenue, which Fran Taylor started in 1946 with a $30 investment. She featured multicolored hand-painted glassware that is highly collectable today. (Courtesy of Robert Evans.)

LANCASTER FESTIVAL. Every summer since 1985 during the last two weeks of July, Lancaster experiences one of its busiest times when the Lancaster Festival is held. Art, music, and culture are everywhere. Thousands of music lovers descend on the grounds of the campus of Ohio University to hear the symphonic orchestra accompany a famous musical entertainer and later see a huge fireworks display.

HEROES' WELCOME. Citizens are gathering at the train station for the arrival of veterans returning home from the Spanish-American War in 1898. Excited fans are sitting atop the train car. The white building at the top is the African Methodist Church on Walnut Street. It was erected in 1869, but in 1914 the building was turned around to face the street.

FORMATION. Friends and family line up to say goodbye to Company I, Ohio Volunteer Infantry. The boys are leaving for duty in Puerto Rico in 1898. (Courtesy of Ohio Glass Museum.)

OFF TO WAR. A large group of men with packed bags await transportation at the Sherman Memorial during World War I. Some 2,000 of these men left, and 80 of them (some young and others not so young) would never return to their hometown.

GAS EXPLOSION. At 6:30 a.m. on January 18, 1892, a gas explosion at the mansion of Judge John Scofield Brasee at the corner of North Columbus and Mulberry Streets rocked the city. Injuries but no deaths occurred. Extensive damage was done to the English Lutheran Church next door. Anna, the wife of the judge, sued the city for $15,000 but lost the case. (Courtesy Fairfield Heritage Association.)

GREEN GRASS OF WYOMING. Lancaster got a taste of the glamorous life in June 1947, when 20th Century Fox arrived with a troop of actors, writers, and technicians. Taking a lunch break from filming on location at the fairgrounds are actors of the movie: Peggy Cummins, Charles Coburn, Robert Arthur, and Lloyd Nolan. Other members of the movie crew have joined them.

FILMING. Lancastrians mill around during the filming of a scene in the movie shot on location at the fairgrounds in 1947. Hundreds were picked to become "movie stars for a day," as many extras were needed for the crowd scene shots of the grandstand. Only a couple of local citizens received speaking parts. (Courtesy of Ohio Glass Museum.)

Judges. These gentlemen are being filmed for the movie that came to town. During the three weeks of filming, the fairgrounds were free to the public, and thousands came to mingle with the movie stars and watch the action. It was estimated that 40,000 townspeople came out on the weekends. (Courtesy of Ohio Glass Museum.)

Movie Stars. The actors pictured here are, from left to right, (first row) Lloyd Nolan and Peggy Cummins; (second row) Geraldine Wall and Robert Arthur. The name of the waiter to the left is unknown. The cast of *The Green Grass of Wyoming* is taking a break from filming to have lunch at a local diner. The film was released in 1948.

LODGE PARADE, 1908. This photograph was taken as the members of various lodges met to march down Main Street. In the background, the sign of the *Gazette* can be seen. This was before the merger of the *Eagle* and the *Gazette* newspapers that came about around 1935. (Courtesy of James Nevins.)

Ten

BUILDINGS OF FAITH AND PLACES OF REST

ST. MARY'S OF THE ASSUMPTION CATHOLIC CHURCH, 1865. The parish was founded in 1820. This is the third Catholic church to be built in Lancaster. The Victorian Gothic structure was completed in 1864 and built of stone, wood, and brick; it holds no steel. The tower bells are lovingly named Joseph, John, and George. The vacant land to the left is where the new courthouse was built.

INTERIOR OF ST. PETER'S LUTHERAN CHURCH. This Gothic Revival–style building was erected in 1875 and dedicated in 1882. The chancel features life-sized wooden statues of Christ and the four evangelists from 1894 that closely resemble copies of Thorvaldsen's works in Copenhagen. Lutheran missionaries came from Pennsylvania in 1804, and the congregation of St. Peter's was incorporated in 1840.

FIRST UNITED METHODIST, 1905. The congregation was organized in a log cabin in 1799. The first building was erected at the site of the current Masonic temple. This present, beautiful Italianate church was erected in 1905 on Wheeling Street.

FIRST PRESBYTERIAN CHURCH OF LANCASTER.
The Lancaster Presbyterian Church was
organized in 1805. There have been five
church buildings erected at the same
North Broad Street location. This one was
completed in 1969, and recycled parts of
the 1892 and 1936 buildings were used in
the chapel and Sunday school rooms.

AFRICAN METHODIST EPISCOPAL CHURCH (AME). In 1810, Scipio Smith, a tin and coppersmith, immigrated to Lancaster. Here he worked for local businessman Samuel Effinger before beginning his own business. Smith founded the AME church in Lancaster about 1825 on land that had been donated by Emanuel Carpenter Jr. He is listed as the first minister.

FOREST ROSE CEMETERY. Once the burial grounds of the German Lutheran Church and the English Lutheran Church were separated in 1882, the city was given the two pieces of property, purchased additional land, and combined both cemeteries to found Forest Rose. This large marble headstone with a cannon relief stands as a silent memorial to those who gave their all during the War of the Great Rebellion.

ELMWOOD CEMETERY. The first burials were held in the East End Burial Grounds (now called Elmwood) in 1838. Many early Lancaster dignitaries are resting peacefully there today, including Judge Philemon Beecher, Gov. William Medill, the elder Shermans, elder Thomas Ewing, H. H. Hunter, Samuel Maccracken, and many other judges and generals from the Civil War era.

THE STONEWALL CEMETERY. The cemetery and 1 acre of planted locust trees was willed to the U.S. president and his successors in 1817. Considered to be one of the finest examples of dry stone masonry in Ohio, the dodecagon-shaped wall was built in 1838. The wall encloses the Nathaniel Wilson Sr. family burial grounds. He emigrated from Cumberland County, Pennsylvania, in 1798.

Visit us at
arcadiapublishing.com

Printed in the USA
CPSIA information can be obtained
at www.ICGtesting.com
LVHW080930071023
760468LV00009B/128